Gary Jones

Paris

First published by Gary Jones in 2016.

This book was professionally typeset on Reedsy.
Find out more at reedsy.com

Contents

1

Introduction

This book is for the traveler who has limited time and want to see the best Paris has to offer in 2 or 3 days.This book is about experiencing the best of the best in a short time.

Paris is an amazing city, and one of the biggest mistakes people make when visiting a great city like Paris is to try and see everything in 2 or 3 days.The problem with this approach is that you end up running from one place to the next and not really experiencing the amazing energy of Paris.You end up being exhausted and wishing you could go home.

The best approach for short stay travelers is to focus on the best the city has to offer.This approach allows you experience the best and really soak up the unique energy of Paris.Take your time and relax.Don't turn travel into a stressful experience.

I hope this little book will help you to make your stay in Paris one of the best experiences of your life.Have a great time in the city of Love! Good Luck!

2

Transportation and Safety

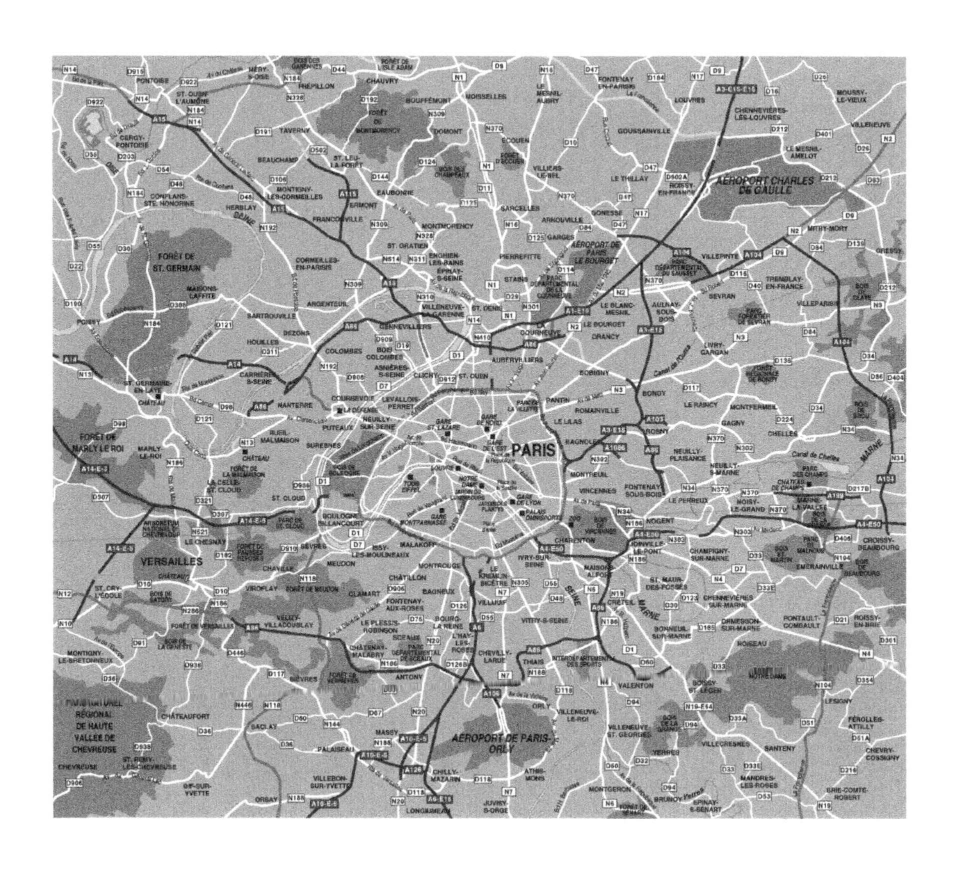

Getting Around Paris

The best way to get into Paris from Charles De Gaulle airport is to take the RER train that has several stops in central Paris and connects with the Metro System(Subway).

Paris International Airport Website
http://www.parisaeroport.fr/en/passengers/access/paris-charles-de-gaulle
Paris International Airport Train Website
http://easycdg.com/ground-transportation/charles-de-gaulle-airport-cdg-to-paris-by-rer-train/
Paris International Airport Map
https://goo.gl/maps/t4LjvrY5Cf92

Since you only have a few days in Paris, I will recommend you use the Paris Metro(Subway) to get around the City.The Metro trains are a quick and easy way to get around the city and avoid traffic jams.The

Paris Metro system has around 300 stations.The Metro (subway) runs every day from 6am to 0:30am.

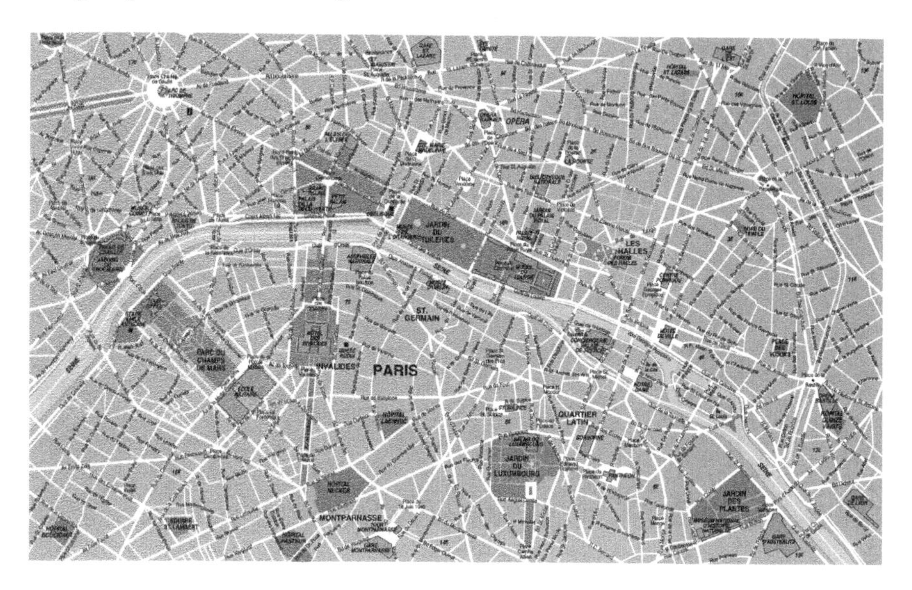

Paris Metro Website
http://www.ratp.fr/en/ratp/c_21879/
visiting-paris/

If you find yourself in a situation in Paris where you can't find a taxi, or it's too late to take the subway then look for a Noctilien(Night bus).These busses run from 0:30am to 5:30 am.

Paris Night Bus Website
http://www.ratp.fr/en/ratp/r_61851/
noctilien-night-bus/

The cheapest way to get around the city is to buy a Paris transport travel card.This card will give you unlimited access to Metro, Bus and RER trains.

If you do decide to take taxis in Paris make sure the Taxi has the red illuminated "Taxi Parisien" sign on the roof and has a taxi meter inside the cab displaying the cost.Don't get into an illegal cab or your journey could end in a bad experience by being asked to pay a lot of money for a short journey.

Paris Transport Website
http://www.ratp.fr/itineraires/en/ratp/recherche-avancee

Safety

Paris is one of the safest cities in Europe when it comes to violent crimes.But crimes like pickpocketing is fairly common.If you are traveling alone be conscious of your surroundings, especially at night.

Let's look at some tips that you can follow to be safe in Paris:

(1)Never leave your bags and valuables unattended in public areas like the bus or metro.

(2)Pickpocketing is fairly common in crowded places like the metro.So make sure your valuables like your wallet and passport is in a safe place.Don't carry too much cash on you and always leave a backup cash or credit card at your hotel.Pickpockets blend in well with the crowd and work in teams.They have been known to pretend to be a romantic couple shopping around.The Louvre Museum is also a very popular spot for pickpockets.So be on cautious!

(3)If you are traveling alone avoid the following areas at night:

-Les Halles, Chatelet, Gare du Nord and Stalingrad.
These areas have been known to have some gang activity.

-The Northern Paris suburbs of Saint-Denis, Aubervilliers, Saint-Ouen.
These areas have been known to have incidents of hate crimes recently so be careful.If you do walk around these areas avoid wearing jewelry or clothing representing any religion since these hate crimes are getting more common in some parts of Paris.

(4)Although Paris is a reasonably safe city, Women should especially be careful walking at night.Don't make too much-prolonged eye contact with men because it could, unfortunately, be seen as a sign of interest.So be aware of this.Remember also that Paris is a world city and that there are some foreign gang elements in France that speaks French fluently.So be cautious of strange men trying to take you to a place you don't know.

(5)Pedestrians should be careful in Paris.Drivers in France are very aggressive so be sure to look twice when crossing a busy road.

(6)If you find yourself in a dangerous situation and you need to call the Police dial "17"

3

Hotels

If you are visiting Paris for a couple of days, you better search for a place to stay. Here is a list of hotels that might strike your fancy.The first group of hotels are for the budget traveler,and the second for people who want to spend a bit more on accommodation.

Budget Hotels

- **Hotel Regyns Montmarte**

Hotel Regyns Montmarte ,is a cosy little hotel in the heart of Montmarte. This hotel has a classic Parisian style hotel, and you will have a classic French style experience if you decide to stay here.

Phone :+33 1 42 54 45 21
Address : 18 Place des Abbesses, 75018 Paris
Website
http://www.paris-hotels-montmartre.com/fr/regyns
Hotel Regyns Montmarte Map
https://goo.gl/maps/zbr3VViXup52

- **Familia Hotel**

The Familia Hotel is a legendary Budget Hotel in Paris.If you are looking for something cosy and traditional, then this is the place for you.

Phone : +33 1 43 54 55 27
Address : 11 Rue des Écoles, 75005 Paris
Familia Hotel Map
https://goo.gl/maps/5dgkggrWEY62

- **Hotel Arvor**

Hotel Arvor is a stylish hotel , but in typical french style they manage to create a homely feeling that makes you feel like you are in a home away from home.

Phone :+33 1 48 78 60 92
Address : 8 Rue Laferrière, 75009 Paris
Website
http://hotelarvor.com/en/
Hotel Arvor Map
https://goo.gl/maps/yVXYaUZzxno

- **Port Royal Hotel**

Port Royal Hotel is an amazing budget hotel in the Latin quarter of Paris.The reputation of this Hotel is legendary, and you will find an extremely clean room and great service.

Phone : +33 1 43 31 70 06
Address : 8 Boulevard de Port-Royal, 75005 Paris
Website
http://www.port-royal-hotel.fr/
Port Royal Hotel Map
https://goo.gl/maps/GPZ20mdqujv

- **Hotel Ecole Centrale**

This hotel has a unique decoration style, and you will see plants and flowers everywhere.They have free wi-fi and all-round great service.The Hotel is very close to the trendy area Marais.

Phone : +33 1 48 04 77 76
Address : 3 Rue Bailly, 75003 Paris
Website
http://paris-marais-hotel.fr/en/accueil.html
Hotel Ecole Centrale Map
https://goo.gl/maps/21SPZd93Ma92

Pricey Hotels

- **Hôtel Plaza Athénée Paris**

It is a hip and an extremely plush hotel that is located near the Eiffel Tower. It has a balcony that replete with red awnings. Inside the hotel, you will be greeted by warm bouquets of flowers.

One of the most sought-after areas in Hôtel Plaza Athénée Paris is the bar. It has an illuminated glass counter that resembles a very large iceberg.

If you need a little bit of rest and relaxation, you should visit the nearby Dior Institut Spa where you will be treated with a bevy of massages using the lush fragrances from the fashion company. Other amenities that you can find in the hotel include a music library that boasts of more than 5,000 tunes and a wine cellar that houses 35,000 different bottles.

Phone : +33 1 53 67 66 65
Address : 25 Avenue Montaigne, 75008 Paris
Website
https://www.dorchestercollection.com/en/paris
/hotel-plaza-athenee/
Hôtel Plaza Athénée Paris Map
https://goo.gl/maps/NnWYwvqHwLp

- **Hotel Therese**

This is one of the very first and unique boutique hotels that you can find in the city of love. Hotel Therese is a favorite among fashion editors and enthusiasts because it is extremely close to the designer stores in the Palais-Royal. It is also near the Musée du Louvre.

The Hotel consists of 43 different rooms. The cheapest ones offer a sense of comfort and warmth even though they are slightly compact. Guests can also relax in the sitting rooms that were inspired by the works of Tom Dixon or Jean Jean Royère.

If you are searching for a room that is more expensive, you will definitely enjoy the classic and innovative architectural designs of Jean-Louis Deniot.

Phone : +33 1 42 96 10 01
Address : 5 Rue Thérèse, 75001 Paris
Website
http://www.hoteltherese.com/en/
Hotel Therese Map
https://goo.gl/maps/L7seRfFzxrB2

- **Four Seasons Hotel George V**

The Four Seasons Hotel George V has been around since 1928. It has lasted throughout the ages because it showed elegance and luxury to its patrons.

Fashionable jet-setters flock towards this hotel because of the several modern amenities that the hotel offers. In addition, the interior design is totally splendid. The marble lobby is lined with eye-catching blossoms. The ceilings are lined with crystal chandeliers, and the walls are covered in fine Flemish tapestries.

Phone : +33 1 49 52 70 00

Address : 31 Avenue George V, 75008 Paris
Website
http://www.fourseasons.com/paris/
Four Seasons Hotel George V Map
https://goo.gl/maps/5uZix9sgM5J2

- **Hotel Caron De Beaumarchais**

The design of the establishment still looks a little bit ancient and medieval. However, that does not mean that it lacks in modern amenities such as stylish bathrooms or internet hotspots.

This boutique hotel only has 19 rooms, and each of them has a classic French design. They are replete faux Louis XVI furnishings, and an intricate arrangement of trompe-l'oeil. The atmosphere of the hotel is very romantic.

Hotel Caron De Beaumarchais also has an indoor spa and a nearby pool that is surrounded by murals of Versailles. If you are feeling a little bit hungry, head over to Le Cinq. This two-star restaurant boasts of divine meals such as red tuna fillet, marinated vegetables and Manjari soufflé.

Address : 12 Rue Vieille du Temple, 75004 Paris
Phone : +33 1 42 72 34 12
Website
http://www.carondebeaumarchais.com/english/index.html
Hotel Caron De Beaumarchais Map
https://goo.gl/maps/LrjFai2P8hM2

4

Historical Sites

Aside from being the City of Light, Paris is also a lovely city rich in culture and history. Paris is lavish in historical and monumental structures that are iconic and breathtaking. More than just the Eiffel Tower, this romantic city is popular for many other wondrous structures that evoke magnificent feelings in tourists and travelers in Paris. Check them out below:

- **Pantheon**

Located in the Latin Quarter, the Pantheon (which means "every god") is a neo-classical monument that is deemed to be the first of its kind. It was originally built as a replacement for the ruined Sainte-Genevieve Church under the order of Louis XV and assigned Jacques-Germain Soufflot as the chief architect. Soufflot combined gothic and classical principles in creating the structure, but all his plans were not carried out when he died just before the church was completed.

The Pantheon was first called as the new Sainte-Genevieve Church, but during the French Revolution, the Revolutionist government turned the massive church into a mausoleum for burying the outstanding Frenchmen that sacrificed their lives for the people. The Pantheon reverted back to being a church until it finally stayed as a place for burial for the martyrs and exceptional French citizens.

Phone : +33 1 44 32 18 00
Address : Place du Panthéon, 75005 Paris
Website
http://www.paris-pantheon.fr/
Pantheon Map
https://goo.gl/maps/1bmf4q5mZmN2

- **La Conciergerie**

The Concergerie has a rich history and has witnessed a thousand years of power play between great politicians and royalties. It was built within a Roman fortress and was part of the Palais de Justice before it was later turned into a court and prison during the French Revolution. La Conciergerie was used by the Revolutionary Tribunal to house their prisoners before their executions.This was the place where Marie Antoinette was kept before she was guillotined.

The Conciergerie is considered as one of the finest pieces of architecture during the Middle Ages. Some of the areas that you should totally visit are the guard room and Gens d'Armes. Drop by the northeastern region to see Paris' first ever public clock. It was installed in the area in 1370.

Phone : +33 1 53 40 60 80
Address : 2 Boulevard du Palais, 75001 Paris

Website
http://www.paris-conciergerie.fr/
La Conciergerie Map
https://goo.gl/maps/w5MLkuhFUSB2

- **Père Lachaise Cemetery**

The Père Lachaise Cemetery was named after Père François de la Chaise, the confessor of Louis XIV. It was established by Napoleon in 1804, built on the site where the Jesuit priest lived, and designed by Alexandre-Théodore Brongniart. It is the most visited Parisian necropolis because of its tombs that are ornamented by monuments of every kind of funerary art style.

Even though it is a cemetery, it is still a fine place for a romantic date. That is because it is revered by many as one of the most poetic graveyards in the world. A lot of influential people are buried in its walls. Fans of The Doors usually pay their respect to Jim Morrison's grave. Literary figures such as Oscar Wilde, Richard Wright and even Molière are buried here.

Cemeteries are usually filled with a lot of grief and sadness. However, you will be surprised to discover that you can find joy in the cemetery's peak while viewing the lavish designs of the crypts.

Phone : +33 1 55 25 82 10
Address : 16 Rue du Repos, 75020 Paris
Website
http://www.pere-lachaise.com/perelachaise.php?lang=en
Père Lachaise Cemetery Map
https://goo.gl/maps/qHb94SQpeCT2

- **Place de la Concorde**

Known for this site's notoriety during the French Revolution, Place de la Concorde was the plaza for the execution of many prominent French. A total of 1119 people were beheaded using the guillotine that was installed in the center of the plaza.

Historical monuments abound the Place de la Concorde, including the statue of King Louis XV, the Liberte, the old obelisk from the temple of Ramses II at Thebes, the statues representing French cities (Bordeaux, Brest, Lille, Lyon, Marseille, Nantes, Rouen and Strasbourg), and the fountains "La fontaine des Mers" and "Elevation of the Maritime."

Address : 75008 Paris
Place de la Concorde Map
https://goo.gl/maps/LkcyR1UAQVq

- **La Sainte-Chapelle**

Located near the Palais de la Cité, this beautiful medieval gothic chapel once housed the relic "Crown of Thorns" before it was relocated to the Notre Dame Cathedral. The chapel is a stunning house of vibrantly colored stained glass windows and majestic chandeliers. This historical site is revered by many as a top-notch Gothic wonder.

The entire area looks very delicate. As you try to traverse the chapel's vast aisles, it feels like you are actually inside a huge palace that is made from colored bits of glass. Its wall paintings and carvings are also a marvel to look at. It was constructed in order to store the crown of thorns that Jesus Christ had worn during his crucifixion. King Louis IX managed to buy this from Constantinople's emperor during the 13th century.

Phone : +33 1 53 40 60 80
Address : 8 Boulevard du Palais, 75001 Paris
Website
http://www.sainte-chapelle.fr/
La Sainte-Chapelle Map
https://goo.gl/maps/XN5TN3cwdHm

- **Opera Garnier(Palais Garnier)**

Originally called the Salle des Capucines because it was located on the Boulevard des Capucines, it was later named Palais Garnier after its architect, Charles Garnier. It is a large opera house for the Paris Opera and can seat 1,979 audiences then and now it can accommodate 2,200 people. This neo-baroque style architectural treasure is now home of the Paris ballet when the Paris Opera relocated to the Opera Bastille in 1989

Phone : +33 1 71 25 24 23
Address : 8 Rue Scribe, 75009 Paris
Website
https://www.operadeparis.fr/en
Opera Garnier Map
https://goo.gl/maps/NTdpB5YPEyE2

- **Arc de Triomphe**

To commemorate the French soldiers, Napoleon commissioned the building of this monumental arch after their victory at the Battle of Austerlitz. This historical triumphal arch is richly engraved with inscriptions that chronicle the French military victories, including the names of the generals and the battles that were fought.

This 164-foot arch was built in order to stir up military dominance and victory against its enemies. You have to understand that Arc de Triomphe was constructed in a time when powerful leaders erect various monuments in order to honor their greatness, as well as to give themselves a massive ego boost.

Arc de Triomphe is a sight to behold because of the majestic sculptures that were carved on its arch. After you have seen the elegance of this massive site, you can head down to the luxurious avenue called the Champs-Elysees.

Phone : +33 1 55 37 73 77
Address : Place Charles de Gaulle, 75008 Paris
Website
http://www.paris-arc-de-triomphe.fr/
Arc de Triomphe Map

https://goo.gl/maps/NCg8fmnGdJw

- **Hôtel de Cluny and Roman Baths**

Hôtel de Cluny is located not far from the Sorbonne in the Latin Quarter. It was built on the ruins of the Gallo-Roman thermal baths, the Thermes de Cluny. The ruins remaining today constitute about one third of the original bath complex.

The hotel, which was once the town house of the abbots of Cluny, is a combination of Gothic and Renaissance art elements when it was rebuilt by Jacques d'Amboise. Today, the hotel houses the Musée du Moyen-Age or Musée de Cluny.

Phone : +33 1 53 73 78 00

Address : 6 Place Paul Painlevé, 75005 Paris
Website
http://www.musee-moyenage.fr/
Hôtel de Cluny and Roman Baths Map
https://goo.gl/maps/jwy6TsPLGns

- **Crypte Archeologique Paris**

Hidden underneath the Notre Dame Cathedral, the Crypte Archeologique of Paris can be accessed by a stairwell in the plaza. It houses the ruins of Lutetia, the Ancient Gallo-Roman town that existed before the place became known as Paris.

Phone : +33 1 55 42 50 10
Address : 7 Parvis Notre-Dame - Pl. Jean-Paul II, 75004 Paris
Website
http://www.crypte.paris.fr/
Crypte Archeologique Paris Map
https://goo.gl/maps/Wo66i3uHtq12

- **The Sorbonne**

The Sorbonne, founded and built in 1257, is one of Europe's oldest universities. It was built originally for theological studies because scholarship at that time was mostly a monastic domain.

It was first known as the Collège de Sorbonne before it was more famously known as the University of Paris. It was strictly a Catholic university until it was placed under Protestant control in the rule of King Francis I.

Phone : +33 1 40 46 22 11
Address : 75005 Paris
Website
http://www.english.paris-sorbonne.fr/
The Sorbonne Map
https://goo.gl/maps/h1d5aKjV32Q2

- **Les Invalides**

Also known as L'Hôtel des Invalides, this structure is a complex of buildings that houses museums and is the site of Napoleon Bonaparte's tomb. It was built in the seventeenth century to serve as a center of recuperation and refuge for injured soldiers under the order of King Louis XIV

Phone : +33 810 11 33 99
Address : 129 Rue de Grenelle, 75007 Paris
Website
http://www.musee-armee.fr/accueil.html
Les Invalides Map
https://goo.gl/maps/KYb2quApbHG2

- **The Latin Quarter**

The Latin Quarter, or Quartier Latin, surrounds the Sorbonne. It is a massive plaza of scholastic activity that houses several institutions of higher education. The name of the place itself is reminiscent of the days of Bohemian Paris.

Address : Latin Quarter, 75005 Paris
The Latin Quarter Map
https://goo.gl/maps/HuMEJ7coFL22

- **Notre Dame Cathedral of Paris**

If this is your first time to visit the city of love, then you should definitely pass by the Notre Dame Cathedral. Disney drew a stellar caricature of this place in their animated film called The Hunchback of Notre Dame. However, the actual cathedral is more marvelous in real life. The entire establishment is filled with dramatic flair because of its Gothic-inspired architecture.

Notre Dame Cathedral's sharp towers, stained glass windows and long spires will surely sweep you off your feet once you see them. A massive Gothic Cathedral built in 1163 in honor of the Virgin Mary. It now houses the "Crown of Thorns" relic, which was once kept in La Sainte-Chapelle. It is a towering structure along the Seine River that is ornate with breathtaking architectural details like the grotesques, gargoyles, and large stained-glass windows.

It had taken a century of extremely harsh labor before this infrastructure was completed. However, the worker's efforts were not in vain because the end result is a beauty to behold.

When you visit this cathedral, do not forget to climb the topmost part of the North Tower. The dazzling view of the city of love will make you realize why the Notre Dame Cathedral is considered as one of the best attractions in the area.

Phone : +33 1 42 34 56 10
Address : 6 Parvis Notre-Dame - Pl. Jean-Paul II, 75004 Paris
Website
http://www.notredamedeparis.fr/
Notre Dame Map
https://goo.gl/maps/q5r7QzPP1i62

- **Palais Royal**

Formerly known as the Palais Cardinal, this beautiful palace was renamed Palais Royal when the cardinal bequeathed the whole place to King Louis XIII. It was almost destroyed by fire in 1871, leaving only the basic structure intact. It was reconstructed in 1876 and now houses the Council of State. The Palais Royal is located between the Opera Garnier and Musee du Louvre.

Phone : +33 1 47 03 92 16
Address : 8 Rue de Montpensier, 75001 Paris
Website
http://www.domaine-palais-royal.fr/
Palais Royal Map
https://goo.gl/maps/vquzsc5BS6P2

- **The Catacombs of Paris**

The Catacombs were former mines before it was transformed into an underground graveyard in the eighteenth century.

These catacombs may not be one of the city's most romantic hot spots, but it is still a good place to visit if you want to have a little bit of a scare. During the 18th century, this labyrinth of bones was once a bustling underground mine. The catacomb of Paris houses a lot of sad tales from fallen soldiers and people who died during the French

Revolution.

More than six million skeletons are kept in this area. If you are fit enough to climb at least 83 steps and if you do not have any claustrophobia, this is a travel destination that you should definitely not miss.

Phone : +33 1 43 22 47 63
Address : 1 Avenue du Colonel Henri Rol-Tanguy,
75014 Paris
Website
http://www.catacombes.paris.fr/en/
homepage-catacombs-official-website
The Catacombs of Paris Map
https://goo.gl/maps/eNRiVzNnUFQ2

- **Hôtel de Ville**

Once called "Place de la Grève," this Renaissance-style structure was a notorious place for executions. Its square has a gory history of beheading, quartering, cooking up, and burning of people at the stake until the installation of a guillotine. The main hall building is decorated with statues that represent famous Parisians and French cities. It now hosts different events throughout the year.

Phone : +33 1 42 76 40 40
Address : Place de l'Hôtel de Ville, 75004 Paris
Hôtel de Ville Map
https://goo.gl/maps/vmvidp52mGN2

- **Eiffel Tower**

The most iconic and popular landmark of Paris is the Eiffel Tower. Named after Gustave Eiffel, this structure was designed as part of a monument competition the Universal Exhibition World Fair and to celebrate the 100th anniversary of the French Revolution. It was originally built to last only 20 years, but it was continually reconstructed and improved to last throughout the last century.

This is considered as one of the most popular landmarks in Paris. That is because it has been featured in numerous television shows, print materials and films. This large iron tower was developed by Gustave Eiffel. It was meant to be presented to the World Exposition in 1889. Unfortunately, the Parisians from the early days did not appreciate the design of the tower. A lot of them even proposed to tear the tower down.

Thankfully, the people started to appreciate the beauty of the Eiffel Tower as time goes by. To this day, more than 200 million tourists have already visited this historical landmark. At night, you should definitely watch the majestic lights that glitter on top of the tower. It would be very difficult to imagine what the city would look like without this very iconic infrastructure.

Phone : +33 892 70 12 39

Address :Champ de Mars, 5 Avenue Anatole France,
75007 Paris
Website
http://www.toureiffel.paris/
Eiffel Tower Map
https://goo.gl/maps/P3F2km29qr72

- **St. Denis Basilica**

One of the oldest places for Christian worship in France, this Catholic basilica is located in St. Denis, a suburb in northern Paris. It is a Gothic structure that is popular for its stained-glass windows and for being a burial site for French monarchs.

Phone : +33 1 48 09 83 54

Address : 1 Rue de la Légion d'Honneur, 93200 Saint-Denis
Website
http://www.saint-denis-basilique.fr/
St. Denis Basilica Map
https://goo.gl/maps/ge3QYFB2ZVz

- **Memorial to the Martyrs of the Deportation**

This memorial place was constructed as a tribute to the 200,000 people who were killed in the Nazi death camps during World War II. It is located across the Notre Dame Cathedral along the banks of the Seine River. The Deportation Memorial was designed by GH Pingusson and evokes a sense of despair and claustrophobia.

Phone : +33 1 46 33 87 56
Address : Allée des Justes de France, 75004 Paris
Website
http://www.cheminsdememoire.gouv.fr/fr/memorial-des-martyrs-de-la-deportation
Memorial to the Martyrs of the Deportation Map
https://goo.gl/maps/EnrhS9yFGGo

- **Louvre**

The Louvre is a historic monument and landmark of Paris. It displays a wealth of artifacts in the Louvre Museum. The building was originally built as a fortress by King Philip II in the 12th century.It was a palace for the household of monarchs until King Louis XIV relocated to the Palace of Versailles and left the Louvre as a primary place for displaying royal collections.

It takes more than a day in order to traverse the entire Louvre and see everything that it has to offer; but for starters, you should definitely go and visit Mona Lisa or the majestic Venus de Milo.

Phone : +33 1 40 20 50 50
Address : 75001 Paris
Website
http://www.louvre.fr/en
Louvre Map
https://goo.gl/maps/SZfqukAccMz

- **Place de la Bastille**

The Bastille prison once stood here, and it's storming on July 14, 1789, signaled the start of the French Revolution. In 1794, the revolutionary authorities beheaded 75 enemies of the state with its guillotine. Today the Bastille Square remains a powerfully symbolic site for Parisians and many marches and demonstrations start or finish here.

Address : Place de la Bastille, 75011 Paris
Place de la Bastille Map
https://goo.gl/maps/PSqyuhPjH592

5

Museums and Galleries

Although many people believe that New York or Berlin has beaten Paris in terms of artistic dominance, the city is still a beautiful place that is teeming with inspiration, colors, museums and passionate artists.What makes Paris different from New York and Berlin is that everyday life is full of artistic expression.

In addition, the city is also dedicated to preserving their artistic inheritance and exposing them to locals and tourists alike. Their galleries and museums house some of the world's most vital and richest masterpieces.

If you are interested in learning more about Paris' artistic legacy, check out some of the best galleries and museums that you should visit. Make sure that you purchase a Paris Museum Pass to make your museum hopping experience easier and fun.

Paris Pass Website
https://www.parispass.com/
- **Louvre Museum**

As mentioned earlier, the Louvre houses a museum that displays a wealth of artifacts. It is also the world's largest, most visited museum. It houses a massive collection of artworks from different centuries of

Parisian and French history, culture, and traditions.

It is also home to artifacts from different historical places around the world and masterpieces of artistic European geniuses.

It takes more than a day in order to traverse the entire Louvre and see everything that it has to offer; but for starters, you should definitely go and visit Mona Lisa or the majestic Venus de Milo.

The Musée du Louvre is considered as one of the most diverse and biggest collection of paintings, decorative items, sculptures and other pieces of artwork from the pre-20th century era. In here, you can witness various masterpieces from renowned artists such as Caravaggio, Vermeer, and a whole lot more.

The historical infrastructure even tells a tale of rich history that spanned from the wonderful medieval ages up to the current era. If you feel weary from viewing paintings and sculptures, you can head towards the nearby Tuileries garden to relax and inhale a breath of fresh air.

Phone : +33 1 40 20 50 50
Address : 75001 Paris
Website
http://www.louvre.fr/en
Louvre Museum Map
https://goo.gl/maps/99s4fJ1Bwa32

- **National Museum of Modern Art (MNAM).**

Pompidou, the National Museum of Modern Art is one of the world's most prestigious centers of modern art collections. It is home to more than 50,000 artworks from popular painters, sculptors, and architects of the 20th century like Picasso, Braque, Pollock. One factor that makes the MNAM a place worth many revisits is their practice of annual re-hanging and re-circulating of artwork displays.

The building itself boasts of innovative and stunning hi-tech architecture courtesy of popular designers Richard Rogers and his friend, Renzo Piano. When the Pompidou was finished in 1977, a lot of the Parisians adored the unique design of the establishment.

However, the vast collection of artworks is more exciting than the actual building. Inside, you will be able to view the masterpieces from contemporary artists such as Picasso and Matisse. On the next aisle, there are surrealist paintings.

In addition, there are also other amenities inside the Centre Georges Pompidou such as children's gallery, performing arts center and a cinema. If you want to bring home some souvenirs, you can visit the nearby design shop and art bookstore. Lastly, fill your hungry stomach in the Georges restaurant once you are finished sightseeing.

Phone : +33 1 53 67 40 00
Address : 11 Avenue du Président Wilson, 75116 Paris
Website
http://www.mam.paris.fr/en/node/155
National Museum of Modern Art Map
https://goo.gl/maps/bbcCAqMsmkR2

- **Musée d'Orsay**

Originally a train station designed by Victor Laloux, the Musée d'Orsay now houses art collections of the 19th and 20th centuries like Monet and Van Gogh. It is located across the Louvre, along the banks of the Seine River.

Phone :+33 1 40 49 48 14
Address : 1 Rue de la Légion d'Honneur, 75007 Paris
Website
http://www.musee-orsay.fr/en/home.html
Musée d'Orsay Map
https://goo.gl/maps/dwzktqLMrMQ2

- **Grand Palais**

The Grand Palais was built for the 1900 Exposition Universelle. It houses galleries of different art collections that are open for temporary exhibits. It also hosts art fairs and galleries for science and natural history.

Website
http://www.grandpalais.fr/en
Grand Palais Map
https://goo.gl/maps/u3qKnX1UMLq

- **Petit Palais**

Located just across the road from the Grand Palais, the Petit Palais showcases art works of about 1.300 from early centuries to the modern 20th century. The admission to the permanent exhibits is free, but the temporary exhibits are free only to visitors under 13 years of age.

Phone :+33 1 53 43 40 00
Address : Avenue Winston Churchill, 75008 Paris
Website
http://www.petitpalais.paris.fr/en
Petit Palais Map
https://goo.gl/maps/zB9dZw96GzH2

- **Musee d'Art Moderne de la Ville de Paris**

Housed in the Palais de Tokyo, the city of Paris' museum of modern art features more than 8,000 contemporary art works of the 20th and 21st centuries. It constantly hosts temporary exhibits, including photography works of modern photography artists.

Phone : +33 1 53 67 40 00
Address : 11 Avenue du Président Wilson, 75116 Paris
Website
http://www.mam.paris.fr/en
Musee d'Art Moderne de la Ville de Paris Map
https://goo.gl/maps/dSmHmG6usKw

- **Cité de l'Architecture et du Patrimoine**

Built as an architecture and heritage museum, it features galleries of life-size mock-ups of facades of different cathedrals and heritage buildings. It also houses a gallery of full-scale copies of stained-glass windows and murals of medieval and Renaissance structures. Another highlight of their exhibits is the walk-in apartment replica of Le Corbusier's Cité Radieuse in Marseille.

Phone : +33 1 58 51 52 00
Address : 1 Place du Trocadéro et du 11 Novembre, 75116 Paris
Website
http://www.citechaillot.fr/en/
Cité de l'Architecture et du Patrimoine Map
https://goo.gl/maps/GTev2B4z5652

- **Musée du Quai Branly**

Located at the banks of the Seine River, this museum houses ethnic arts of non-European cultures. It features a treasure of contemporary indigenous art and 10th century anthropomorphic statues.

Phone : +33 1 56 61 70 00
Address : 37 Quai Branly, 75007 Paris
Website
http://www.quaibranly.fr/en/

Musée du Quai Branly Map
https://goo.gl/maps/JfJYWSuhxcv

- **Musée du Moyen-Age**

Also known as Musée de Cluny, this museum is housed within the Hôtel de Cluny. This gallery is dedicated to the art works of the medieval period. Its grounds also feature a garden that mimics the aromatic and medicinal gardens of the medieval times.

True to its name, the National Medieval Museum is a gallery that houses a vast collection of relics from the medieval times. It aims to explore the types of art that sprang during this era and retells the stories of how the people live during the great "Moyen Age."

The most prized possession in the museum is a tapestry called The Lady and The Unicorn. It was created in the 15th century and it gained immense popularity because of its symbolism and a striking array of colors.

Phone :+33 1 53 73 78 00
Address : 6 Place Paul Painlevé, 75005 Paris
Website
http://www.musee-moyenage.fr/
Musée du Moyen-Age Map
https://goo.gl/maps/WBxQo6ZiCXD2

- **Rodin Museum**

This museum features an extensive garden of sculptures by the French sculptor Auguste Rodin.

As you view some of his works such as the Balzac, Burghers of Calais, and the Gates of Hell, you will discover how this man revolutionized the art of sculpting during the 1900s. It is also exciting to learn how he frequently reused some of his previous sculptures in his next works.

The Musée National Rodin also houses some of the masterpieces from his student, Camille Claudel. The chapel is usually busy with temporary exhibitions. If you are looking for a place to relax, there is a lovely café located near the garden.

Phone : +33 1 44 18 61 10
Address : 79 Rue de Varenne, 75007 Paris
Website
http://www.musee-rodin.fr/en
Rodin Museum Map
https://goo.gl/maps/ngcGKrtPZyN2

- **Musée Carnavalet**

Also known as the Museum of Paris History, the Carnavalet Museum houses collections of historical artifacts and items that trace Paris' complex history in over 100 chronological rooms. Admission to the exhibits is free for all visitors.

Phone : +33 1 44 59 58 58
Address : 16 Rue des Francs Bourgeois, 75003 Paris
Website
http://www.carnavalet.paris.fr/en/homepage
Musée Carnavalet Map
https://goo.gl/maps/QggUv5Pq5tT2

- **Musée du Luxembourg**

Located in the luxuriant Luxembourg Gardens, the Luxembourg museum is one of Europe's oldest museums. It hosts temporary exhibits annually and focuses on paintings by French artists.

Phone : +33 1 40 13 62 00
Address : 19 Rue de Vaugirard, 75006 Paris
Website
http://en.museeduluxembourg.fr/
Musée du Luxembourg Map
https://goo.gl/maps/nQEhrqzDpbo

- **Musee Jacquemart-André**

The Jacquemart-André museum was founded by art collector, Edouard André and his artist wife Nélie Jacquemart. Its galleries focus on the works of French painters of the 18th and 19th century.

Phone : +33 1 45 62 11 59
Address : 158 Boulevard Haussmann, 75008 Paris
Website
http://www.musee-jacquemart-andre.com/en

Musee Jacquemart-André Map
https://goo.gl/maps/o4TeCEXUA4J2

- **Musée des Arts Décoratifs**

This decorative arts museum features one of the world's massive collections of design art. The primary focus of the museum is the French furniture and tableware. There are other galleries that are categorized by glass, drawings, toys, and wallpaper themes.

Phone : +33 1 44 55 57 50
Address : 107 Rue de Rivoli, 75001 Paris
Website
http://www.lesartsdecoratifs.fr/en/
Musée des Arts Décoratifs Map
https://goo.gl/maps/artmu9jWNX42

6

Restaurants

The city of Paris is a haven for people who enjoy eating a wide variety of dishes. Aside from the famous culinary dishes from France, most restaurants in the city also serve specialty meals from other countries.

The chefs here can replicate your favorite dishes to make you feel closer to home, but they also add a little bit of a twist to each of them to make you appreciate the culture in Paris.

A lot of people think that the city is all about fine dining. Well, it is true that numerous five-star restaurants reside in this place. However, that does not mean that you cannot find some bistros that offer delicious meals at a lower cost. Here is a list of the best eateries, cafés and restaurants that you should definitely visit in Paris:

- **Boco**

Boco is a small chain of eateries that is located along the heart of the city. The famous three-star chefs such as Regis Marcon and Anne-Sophie Pic were the ones who developed the recipes that were placed in the restaurant's menu.

Most of their main dishes, appetizers and desserts were all made from organic ingredients so you have an assurance that what you will eat is fresh, delicious and healthy. Furthermore, their packaging is also eco-friendly. True to its name, this restaurant serves most of its dishes in reusable glass jars.

When you visit this place, you should definitely try Chef Pic's coddled eggs, Chef Renaut's mushroom and polenta lasagna, or Chef Philippe's mouth-watering pistachio crumble topped with a thick cream made from black sesame.

Phone :+33 1 42 61 17 67
Address : 3 Rue Danielle Casanova, 75001 Paris
Website
http://www.boco.fr/en/
Boco Map
https://goo.gl/maps/PGPWWTGTZpJ2

- **Relais d'Entrecôte**

If you are looking for a charming and hassle-free restaurant, this joint is ideal for you. Relais d'Entrecôte is famous for its rich steak frites dish. It is served with a secret sauce that will make your mouths water.

Do not be fooled if your first serving seems a little bit scant. The wait staff in the area is willing to provide you with second helpings of your dish if you want more.Aside from their famous steak frites, you will also enjoy the restaurant's light ambience, brasserie-inspired interior decorations and very accommodating waiters.

Phone : +33 1 46 33 82 82
Address :101 Boulevard du Montparnasse, 75006 Paris
Website
http://www.relaisentrecote.fr/
Relais d'Entrecôte Map
https://goo.gl/maps/Hcyj6j2YkK92

- **Verjus**

This exclusive restaurant is built by an American couple who were famous for their dinner club called the Hidden Kitchen. This place offers a private haven for romantic couples to enjoy each other's company while they are in the city of love.

The menu of Verjus consists of top-notch dishes that are made from seasonal and well-picked produce. If you are searching for a nice place where you can eat fried chicken, this is the restaurant that you should visit; and if you need to enjoy a bottle of fine spirits, feel free to peruse some of their liquor collections in their very own wine bar.

Phone : +33 1 42 97 54 40
Address : 52 Rue de Richelieu, 75001 Paris
Website
http://verjusparis.com/

Verjus Map
https://goo.gl/maps/9XU9tjwNG662

- **Huitrerie Regis**

Huitrerie Regis is located in the middle along Saint Germain des Pres. This is the finest establishment to visit in Paris if you are craving for fresh oysters. That is because their seafood ingredients directly came from the country's Marennes-Oléron area which is located on the coasts of the Atlantic.

Depending on the season, they also serve prawns and sea urchins with bread on the side. You can complement your undersea dishes with a nice bottle of white wine from the Loire valley. The atmosphere of the place is also warm, so you can greatly enjoy your bivalve-centric meals.

Phone : +33 1 44 41 10 07
Address : 3 Rue de Montfaucon, 75006 Paris
Website
http://huitrerieregis.com/
Huitrerie Regis Map
https://goo.gl/maps/b52XjRwCJDv

- **Macéo**

Maceo is operated by Mark Williamson – an English gentleman who also runs the popular local establishment called Willi's Wine Bar. Upon entering the restaurant, you will be greeted with its fine interior decorations that are composed of oxblood walls and floors that are made of parquet. You will also have a stunning view of the city's famous site called Palais Royal.

Chef Thierry Bourbonnais, the one who plans the menu of Macéo, offers several vegetable meals for the hungry vegetarian tourists. You will surely enjoy his scallop dish that is marinated using seaweed oil. The restaurant also serves a healthy plate of sea bass that is replete with mage toute, spicy bulghur and baby carrots. Lastly, they have a vast collection of vintage wines and spirits.

Phone : +33 1 42 97 53 85
Address : 15 Rue des Petits Champs, 75001 Paris
Website
http://www.maceorestaurant.com/Menu.html
Macéo Map
https://goo.gl/maps/7aA9v1udaQr

- **La Cantine de la Cigale**

Located in Pigalle, this place offers a fine array of specialty dishes from the south-west region of France. The restaurant is owned by bistro expert Christian Etchebest.

This cozy place is ideal for those worn-out travelers who are looking for a place to rest after an intense shopping spree. La Cantine de la Cigale's menu is replete with affordable but large portions of paâté, sausage and white bean platter, cherry jams, Mirabelle tarts, and a whole lot more.

Phone : +33 1 55 79 10 10
Address : 124 Boulevard de Rochechouart, 75018 Paris
Website
http://www.cantinelacigale.fr/
La Cantine de la Cigale Map
https://goo.gl/maps/N1hNQdxJHb22

- **Le Coq Rico**

A French cuisine restaurant located at the top of Montmartre butte that specializes in delicious French chicken recipes. From breakfast to dinner, you will enjoy the assortment of homely meals that are worth savoring.

Phone : +33 1 42 59 82 89
Address : 98 Rue Lepic, 75018 Paris
Website
http://en.lecoqrico.com/
Le Coq Rico Map
https://goo.gl/maps/J7j8xpBcAhz

- **Bistro Volnay**

Located near the Opera Garnier, Bistro Volnay is popular with businessmen, Parisians, and tourists alike. Their art deco-inspired place makes it a very warm and inspiring spot to eat, relax, and enjoy.

Phone : +33 1 42 61 06 65
Address : 8 Rue Volney, 75002 Paris
Website
http://www.bistro-volnay.fr/
Bistro Volnae Map
https://goo.gl/maps/Pfzsy99NZNp

- **Chez L'Ami Jean**

This is a well-known Basque venue restaurant for their tasty and diverse French recipes that are very popular. From meat to seafood, you will find any dish in their menu very much worth a try.

Phone : +33 1 47 05 86 89
Address : 27 Rue Malar, 75007 Paris
Website
http://lamijean.fr/

Chez L'Ami Jean Map
https://goo.gl/maps/xVo6EaXtqPo

- **La Pulpéria**

The perfect place for meat lovers, this restaurant is known for their diverse menus that change every day. The meat recipes are cooked flavorfully and look sinfully indulging.

Phone : +33 1 40 09 03 70
Address : 11 Rue Richard Lenoir, 75011 Paris
Website
http://lapulperiaparis.fr/en
La Pulpéria Map
https://goo.gl/maps/LDdedcmysvC2

-
- **Breizh Café**

This crêperie is not a regular dessert station. Their choices of crepe fillings may be limited, but they use ingredient of the highest quality, and they offer a savory sea-side experience with their seafood recipes.

Phone : +33 1 42 72 13 77
Address : 109 Rue Vieille du Temple, 75003 Paris
Website
http://breizhcafe.com/fr/
Breizh Café Map
https://goo.gl/maps/uGdxHcE8Wam

- **Le Flamboire**

If you love barbecues, then this is the place to eat. This is where meat lovers flock to eat and enjoy flavorful and savory grilled meat dishes.

Phone : +33 6 95 01 77 38
Address : 54 Rue Blanche, 75009 Paris
Website
http://leflamboire.com/en/
Le Flamboire Map
https://goo.gl/maps/1fYhusjG4WR2

- **Frenchie To Go**

A takeaway sandwich bar that you will truly love. The queues are long though, so you have to be patient to get a bite of their well-known snacks.

Phone : +33 1 40 26 23 43
Address : 9 Rue du Nil, 75002 Paris
Website
http://www.frenchietogo.com/
Frenchie To Go Map
https://goo.gl/maps/jw9ycREXzT62

- **Urfa Dürüm**

A Kurdish sandwich shop that is said to be the best place for eating street food in Paris. This small but welcoming place will make you anticipate for their delicious Lahmacun and Dürüm.

Phone : +33 1 48 24 12 84
Address : 58 Rue du Faubourg Saint-Denis, 75010 Paris
Website
https://www.facebook.com/pages/Urfa-Durum/240014419359256
Urfa Dürüm Map
https://goo.gl/maps/HezFAoykrbN2

- **Miznon**

Street food never looked so good in Paris. Miznon is a restaurant that serves casual western-style French foods that are worth trying, particularly their pita sandwiches.

Phone : +33 1 42 74 83 58
Address : 22 Rue des Ecouffes, 75004 Paris
Website
https://www.facebook.com/miznonparis/
Miznon Map
https://goo.gl/maps/kAXsbuYs45C2

7

Shopping Districts

Your trip to the city of love will never be complete without a little bit of shopping. As you work your way around the busy streets of the city, you will discover that a lot of the locals find it so easy to look so fabulous and fashionable. It is no wonder that this city is still a center for everything couture. Next to historical landmarks, the shopping districts in Paris draw millions of tourists every year.

Whether you are a fashion victim, bargain hunter, window shopper or high-fashion diva, there is always a shop that will surely satiate your desires. Check them out below.

- **Sophie Sacs**

This boutique is popular for its low prices and huge sales, especially on bags. This establishment has been up and running ever since it opened in 1976, and has remained popular and crowded by people from all over Paris.

Phone : +33 1 45 48 00 69
Address : 149 Rue de Rennes, 75006 Paris
Website
http://www.sophiesacs.com/
Sophie Sacs Map
https://goo.gl/maps/zSMYWSkXGXw

- **La Boutique de Louise**

Specializing in girly accessories, this boutique is popular for its affordable but cute accessory items like printed cushions, necklaces and pendants, bracelets, and fun items for your home.

Phone : +33 1 45 49 07 92
Address :32 Rue du Dragon, 75006 Paris
Website
http://www.laboutiquedelouise.com/shop/
La Boutique de Louise Map
https://goo.gl/maps/DathuAzwBhH2

- **Beau Travail**

A designer boutique formed by four aspiring and talented local designers who opened their couture creations to the public in the heights of Belleville. Displaying their creations with amazing price tags, Beau Travail, however, is only open to the public on schedule or by appointment.

Phone : +33 1 43 67 33 86
Address : 131 Rue de Bagnolet, 75020 Paris
Website
http://www.beautravail.fr/
Beau Travail Map
https://goo.gl/maps/C9hNUj6BAR92

- **Haili**

Established by former stylist Patricia Wang, this boutique features designer clothes of diverse varieties. She also carries new designer names from other parts of Europe every season. Additionally, Patricia herself can happily offer styling advice to her customers.

Phone : +33 1 40 47 54 86
Address : 56 Rue Daguerre, 75014 Paris, France
Haili Map
https://goo.gl/maps/QrRrtzxryE52

- **Paperdolls**

This boutique by Candy Miller offers everything girly from chic apparels, handbags, and shoes. Her boutique features works from independent designers only. The highlight of this shop is the apartment-lie interior that divides the place into apartment rooms like a dining room, bathroom, and living room.

Phone : +33 1 42 51 29 87
Address : 5 Rue Houdon, 75018 Paris
Website

http://www.paperdolls.fr/en/
Paperdolls Map
https://goo.gl/maps/uku1xWSBWxx

- **Anne Willi**

This boutique by Anne Willi is great for finding and shopping for items that match different curves and personalities. The designs and materials are contemporary and will fit any occasion.

Phone : +33 1 48 06 74 06
Address : 13 Rue Keller, 75011 Paris
Website
http://www.annewilli.com/
Anne Willi Map
https://goo.gl/maps/a8xPpdjyxAu

- **Annabel Winship**

Popular shoe boutique that features designs that think out of the box. If you quirky and fantastical shoe designs are your thing, this shop will be worth a visit.

Phone : +33 1 71 37 60 46
Address : 29 Rue Dragon, 75006 Paris
Website
http://www.annabelwinship.com/stores.html
Annabel Winship Map
https://goo.gl/maps/vMab1USXCzt

Shopping Areas

Let's take a look at some of the best areas in Paris to go shopping.If you just want to take a walk and do some window shopping then I have a few suggestions for you:

- **Louvre-Tuileries and the district of Faubourg Saint-Honoré**

These places are ideal for tourists who are looking for top-notch cosmetics, designer clothes, and even stylish home furnishings. The district of Faubourg Saint-Honoré is always teeming with people because this is where most of the city's top fashion stores are placed. These include Yves Saint Laurent, Versace and even Hermes.

However, you can also search for popular concept shops here.

On the other hand, the Boulevard Haussmann is located in the neighborhood of Louvre-Tuileries. This is considered as the department store region of Paris.

Address : 113 Rue de Rivoli, 75001 Paris
Louvre-Tuileries and the district of Faubourg Saint-Honoré Map

https://goo.gl/maps/a44WmPjLdNP2

- **The Avenue of Montaigne and des Champs-Elysées**

These two avenues form one of Paris' most sizzling fashion junctures. Legendary brands such as Chanel or Dior line the streets of Avenue Montaigne. Meanwhile Champs- Elysées showcases luxury brands and global chains such as Zara and Louis Vuitton. Both of these avenues are ideal if you are searching for the trendiest chain stores and designer items.

The Avenue of Montaigne and des Champs-Elysées Map
https://goo.gl/maps/C16RJ5MrE4K2

- **Paris Flea Markets**

The most popular and largest flea market in the city of love is called Saint-Ouen flea market. This area has been around since the 1900s. It is located in the northernmost part of Paris. You can visit this place if you want to search for antique home furnishings, oddball objects, vintage apparel and discounted shoes.

Since this is a flea market, one should expect that every inch of the street will be filled with a lot of people during the weekends. So if you want to shop in peace and experience the beauty of the surroundings, it is best if you visit the place during weekends.

Paris Flea Markets Map
https://goo.gl/maps/78GXjbJsHmA2

- **Avenue des Ternes**

Avenue des Ternes is a shopping hub that is not yet extremely popular with the tourists. This means that you can easily get first dibs on the rarest and most fashionable pieces of apparel that are available.

Even though the avenue does not attract a lot of tourists, it does not mean that the place is barren.

It is also a busy and colorful avenue because locals tend to shop here. Aside from clothing, you will find stores that sell home appliances, books, films, music and food. When you get tired from walking and buying, you can take a break in the nearby brasseries, coffee shops and bakeries.

Avenue des Ternes Map
https://goo.gl/maps/zqH5hjp6pP72

- **Montmartre**

Similar to the flea market, Montmartre is also replete with stores that sell affordable pieces of jewelry, shoes, and clothing. The best places to visit are rue des Abbesses, rue Houdon, as well as rue des Martyrs.

If you want to find the cheapest deals, you can head towards Montmartre's eastern region where the working class neighborhood of Barbès is located. In here, you will find a large department store called Tati. This place offers quality apparel with huge discounts.

Montmartre Map
https://goo.gl/maps/vLvL3bcCC7p

- **The Marais**

Once a historical area, the quarters of the Marais have become a center for shoppers with a passion for unique and eclectic fashionable items. In addition, you will also find a load of antique objects and fine pieces of artwork in this place. For art enthusiasts, one of the most highly recommended areas to visit is Place de Vosges.

For people who have an eye for fine jewelry, they can shop at boutiques such as Satellite located near Rue des Francs-Bourgeois. And if you are looking for the next fashion trends, head down towards Rue des Rosiers.

The Marais Map
https://goo.gl/maps/p2g3rDoyEHH2

- **Opéra & Grand Boulevards**

Located in the heart of Opéra & Grand Boulevards are two of the most sought-after department stores in the city- Galeries Lafayetteand the Printemps. Over the years, these large behemoths have built a vast neighborhood of discount shops around them. The most ideal stores in the area are located in the northernmost boulevards such as rue de Provence and rue Caumartin. They sell shoes, jewelry and clothes at extremely affordable prices.

Opéra & Grand Boulevards Map
https://goo.gl/maps/GSedeuFY7ax

8

Paris Bars

- **Silencio**

Silencio is hard to put in words, but in typical French style it's something truly unique.It could be described as a cross between an art nightclub and members only bar.The club is located underground and has a stage and a smoking room.Before midnight, only members of the club is allowed,but after midnight its free to go in for a limited number of people.A night at Silencio is something you will always remember.

Phone : +33 1 40 13 12 33
Address : 142 Rue Montmartre, 75002 Paris
Silencio Website
http://silencio-club.com/en
Silencio Map
https://goo.gl/maps/ZFUXW4yiHp92

- **Candelaria**

You will find Candelaria in a narrow street in Marais area of Paris.In the front of Candelaria, you can buy Mexican snacks like Tacos.However, if you go through the back door of Candelaria, you will find a fantastic cocktail bar.

Phone : +33 7 53 79 68 25
Address : 52 Rue de Saintonge, 75003 Paris
Candelaria Website
http://www.quixotic-projects.com/venue/candelaria
Candelaria Map
https://goo.gl/maps/yqZfnV9KEs72

- **Charlie**

If you want to combine cocktails and art, then go the Charlie.The bar is a trendy up-and-coming hang out in Paris.Charlie has art exhibitions and live music that create a unique atmosphere.Charlie is another one of those places where you walk away thinking you will only experience a place like that in Paris.

Phone : +33 1 53 33 02 67
Address : 29 Rue de Cotte,Paris

Charlie Website
https://www.facebook.com/bierrea2balles
Charlie Map
https://goo.gl/maps/LD9x5iR68uj

9

Coffee

People think about many things when they come to Paris, but one thing they always dream about is having an amazing cup of coffee in one of Paris's best coffee shops.I have made a list of some of the best and unique coffee experiences in Paris:

- **Café des 2 Moulins**

This coffee shop gained immense popularity among tourists when it appeared in Jean-Pierre Jeunet's cult movie called Amélie. Even though it has been more than a decade since the film's release, this is still a popular tourist destination. That is because the café's ambience is very warm and cozy.

You will surely enjoy its vintage atmosphere, comfortable sitting room and relaxing cup of coffee. And once you are finished with this place, feel free to immerse yourself in the colorful market outside the café.

Phone : +33 1 42 54 90 50
Address : 15 Rue Lepic, 75018 Paris
Website
https://goo.gl/maps/rAiAADoBDmA2
Café des 2 Moulins Map
https://goo.gl/maps/rAiAADoBDmA2

- **La Caféothèque**

The name of this establishment means "coffee library" in English. True to its name, La Caféothèque is a highly recommended place for coffee enthusiasts who want to veer away from the cups of espresso at Starbucks. This shop imports their coffee beans from various plantations outside the country.

There is a large coffee roaster at the shop's front, and the scents of the beans always fill the place with delicious aroma. These raw ingredients are brewed well by adept baristas. In addition, they only use the finest espresso machines from the popular maker named La Marzocco.

La Caféothèque is located across Ile Saint-Louis. It is owned by Guatemalan coffee expert named Gloria Montenegro.

Phone : +33 1 53 01 83 84
Address : 52 Rue de l'Hôtel de ville, 75004 Paris
Website
http://www.lacafeotheque.com/
La Caféothèque Map
https://goo.gl/maps/ZjAZDrnJY5K2

- **Café de Flore**

This little coffee shop was once a cozy hub where intellects and artists gather and share ideas with their peers. The author, Charles Maurras, got the inspiration for his novel Au Signe de Flore in this place. Poets such as Guillaume Apollinaire and Louis Aragon sought refuge at Café de Flore when they felt the need to scribble some lines and verses. Even American authors such as Trauman Capote and Arthur Koestler even visited this humble coffee shop.

These days, Café de Flore is still a place where you can sip your favorite blend of coffee, meet fellow intellectuals and discuss some ideas with them.

Phone : +33 1 45 48 55 26
Address : 172 Boulevard Saint-Germain, 75006 Paris
Website

http://cafedeflore.fr/
Café de Flore Map
https://goo.gl/maps/5ymDiGCDHDS2

- **Telescope Coffee**

This shop serves amazing coffee.The coffee shop has a minimalist style, and you won't find many better places drink excellent coffee in a very relaxing environment.The people who run this store take their coffee very seriously, and if you are a bit of a coffee addict like me then you will love this place.

Address : 5 Rue Villedo, 75001 Paris
Website
http://www.telescopecafe.com/
Telescope Coffee Map
https://goo.gl/maps/BApM315jm7K2

- **The Broken Arm**

The Broken Arm is a Scandinavian style coffee shop in the trendy Marais area.The owners combine their three passions of coffee,design and fashion.The coffee served in the Broken arm is excellent and has an edgy atmosphere.

Phone : +33 1 44 61 53 60
Address : 12 Rue Perrée, 75003 Paris
Website
http://the-broken-arm.com/en/
The Broken Arm Map
https://goo.gl/maps/McVTdjPjjiP2

- **Cafe Le Look**

If you like a vintage cafe with a lot of character, then go and drink a cup of coffee at Le Look.This place has an amazing breakfast and also serve beer.

Phone : +33 9 50 10 20 31
Address : 17 Rue Martel, 75010 Paris
Website
https://cafelelook.wordpress.com/
Cafe Le Look Map
https://goo.gl/maps/ddKTmbrNLQK2

10

Sample 3 Day Itinerary

Try this 3-day sample itinerary to get the most out of your Paris experience:

Day 1:

Hop on the sightseeing bus to see all the iconic landmarks such as the Pantheon. Visitors can hop on and off while the ticket is valid.You have unlimited use of the ticket over 1 or 2 days. Other sites to see for this tour are the Louvre, the Eiffel Tower and many others.

Walk around the city and hop on a taxi to see the the Bastille, the Picasso Museum and have a cup of coffee at the The Broken Arm. Have dinner and cocktails at Candelaria.

- **Day 2:**

Go to the trendy Marais area.Walk around and see the Bastille, the Picasso Museum and have a cup of coffee at the The Broken Arm. Have dinner and cocktails at Candelaria.

- **Day 3**

Go to the Avenue of Montaigne and des Champs-Elysées. Have a fantastic day of shopping and enjoy the fashion experience of a lifetime.After shopping go to Montmartre and see the Basilica of the Sacred Heart of Paris(Sacre Coeur).Have a cup of coffee at the famous Cafe des 2 Moulins in Montmartre.

11

Conclusion

I want to thank you for reading this book!I sincerely hope that you received value from it!

against the publisher for any reparation, damages, or monetary loss due to the information herein, either directly or indirectly.

The information herein is offered for informational purposes solely, and is universal as so. The presentation of the information is without contract or any type of guarantee assurance.

The trademarks that are used are without any consent, and the publication of the trademark is without permission or backing by the trademark owner. All trademarks and brands within this book are for clarifying purposes only and are the owned by the owners themselves, not affiliated with this document.

Made in United States
Orlando, FL
09 January 2022